Simple Yet Delicious Halogen Oven Cookbook

Easy Yet Tasty Halogen Oven Recipes for The Whole Family

BY - Stephanie Sharp

License Notes

wwwwwwwwwwwwwwwwwwwwwwwwwwwwwwwwwwww

Table of Contents

Introduction

This comprehensive cookbook is going to share with you some tips and tricks associated with most of the Halogen oven models. There are old family favorites in this book, many new dishes that have been created and tested, plus enticing, colorful photographs of the recipes.

Halogen Oven Cookbook also features recipes specifically designed one or two persons and complete meals that can be prepared without you having to use the conventional hob. The halogen oven user's community is growing large so grab your copy today and be a part of that community.

Refried Bean Quesadilla

On those days when you crave Mexican food, this recipe will come in handy.

Serves: 2

Time: 25 minutes

Ingredients:

- cheddar cheese (4 tbsp, grated)
- jalapeño pepper (1, sliced, de seeded)
- pepper (1/2, sliced, red)
- tomato (1, diced)
- tortillas (4, flour)
- beans (6 oz, refried)
- olive oil (1/2 tbsp)
- onion (1/2, sliced, red)
- Sea salt & pepper (ground)

Directions:

1. Place the red onion and olive oil onto a round tray on the lower rack of your halogen oven and cook for 5 minutes at 500 degrees F.

2. Add the refried beans ad mix, then cook for approx. 3 minutes. Mixture should be thoroughly heated. Remove from oven then add to a medium bowl.

3. Place a tortilla onto an oven tray. Spread ½ of the refried beans on it. Top using cheese, ½ chicken, tomatoes, jalapeño, and peppers.

4. Place the tray onto a low rack of halogen oven then cook for approx., 6 minutes at 500F. Add another tortilla, forming a sandwich, then cook for another minute.

5. Remove the tortilla from oven and keep warm while you cook the second quesadilla. Slice them into quarters then serve with tomatoes and lettuce.

Tomato Chicken

This is one of the easiest meals you'll ever make.

Serves: 4

Time: 1 hour & 15 minutes

Ingredients:

- onion (1, sliced, large)
- olive oil (1/4 cup)
- potatoes (2, quartered, large)
- garlic cloves (4, crushed)
- tomato paste (1 can)
- chicken thighs (4-6, firm)
- lemon (1, juice only)
- Sea salt (coarse)
- Black pepper (ground)

Directions:

1. Preheat the halogen oven to 375 degrees F.

2. Place the garlic, tomato paste, lemon juice, and olive oil into a medium bowl. Add the sea salt & black pepper, as desired.

3. Arrange the potatoes and chicken evenly into a baking dish.

4. Pour the tomato paste over the potatoes and chicken then spread evenly. Place onions over the tomato paste.

5. Use aluminum foil to cover the dish then bake for approx. 45 minutes.

6. As chicken is nearly done, remove the aluminum foil. Broil long enough that the onions brown. Serve hot.

Oven Fried Potatoes

These potatoes are seasoned simply, and they make a super side dish for any meat & potato meal.

Serves: 5

Time: 1 hour & 5 minutes

Ingredients:

- Six or potatoes (6-7, large)

For dressing

- Garlic cloves (3, chopped, crushed)
- basil (1, small bunch, chopped, fresh)
- lemon (1/2, juice only)
- olive oil (3-4 tbsp)
- pepper (several dashes, paprika and pepper flakes red)

Directions:

1. Preheat halogen oven to 350 degrees F.

2. Wash the potatoes and peel them then place them dry.

3. Cut in ¼" slices then prepare all the ingredients. Mix thoroughly then pour dressing on potatoes.

4. Evenly toss potatoes distribute evenly.

5. Bake the potatoes and dressing for approx., 40 minutes potatoes should be golden. Serve hot.

Lamb & Roasted Veggies

Rosemary and lamb work perfectly together.

Serves: 3-5

Time: 70 minutes

Ingredients:

- rosemary (1 tsp, dried)
- chilies (1/2 tsp, chopped)
- garlic cloves (3-4, crushed)

For seasoning

- rosemary sprigs (2-3 sprigs)
- onions (2, red)
- Cooking spray, olive oil
- semolina (2-3 tsp)
- paprika (2-3 tsp)
- potatoes (8, medium)
- potatoes (2, sweet)
- lamb (1 leg)
- olive oil (3 tbsp)

Directions:

1. Mix the olive oil, rosemary, seasonings, garlic together, chili and creating a paste. Then rub the paste over the lamb.

2. Place onto a lower oven rack then cook at 445 degrees F for approx., 15 minutes.

3. Cut the potatoes then steam for approx., 10 minutes then drain them. Return to an empty pan then add the paprika and semolina. Cover pan.

4. Shake to fluff up ingredients and to coat veggies using seasoning.

5. Place the potatoes around the lamb then use the olive oil spray on them. Cut the onions in half then place them using the rest of the vegetables, with the sprigs of rosemary.

6. Cook for an additional 10 more minutes then turn oven down to 375 degrees F. Cook for around 45 minutes. Potatoes and meat should be cooked as you desire. Serve hot.

Chipotle Honey Ribs

These Chipotle Honey Ribs are spicy, sweet and tender.

Serves: 6

Time: 3 hours & 15 minutes

Ingredients:

- Ribs (5-6 lbs., trimmed at market)
- Bottled Honey Chipotle BBQ Sauce

Directions:

1. Slather the BBQ sauce on all sides of the ribs then wrap them into foil.

2. Marinate for approx., several hours, then heat halogen oven to 350 degrees F. Place wrapped ribs inside then bake for approx., 1 & ½ hours.

3. Cook while constantly every 15 minutes or so to see whether meat is withdrawing from the bone.

4. After that happens, remove the aluminum foil then brush the extra sauce onto ribs. Bake for approximately ½ hour longer.

5. Remove from oven then allow to rest for ½ hour. Serve warm.

Chicken Parmesan

This recipe for chicken parmesan can be the perfect side in your family meal, with a salad or spaghetti.

Serves: 4

Time: 35 minutes

Ingredients:

- pasta sauce (12 oz)
- Parmesan cheese (grated, preferred amount)
- mozzarella (8 oz, shredded)
- breadcrumbs (seasoned)
- Italian dressing (low-fat)
- chicken breasts (4, frozen)

Directions:

1. Dip the pieces of chicken into Italian dressing then roll them into the breadcrumbs.

2. Place chicken onto a lined pan then cook approx., 6-8 minutes on each side, until they are done then open the halogen oven.

3. Spoon more sauce onto pieces then sprinkle them using cheese then cook for 2-3 more minutes and serve hot.

Veggie Chili

This Chili is satisfying and filling and ready in less than an hour.

Serves: 1-2

Time: 50 minutes

Ingredients:

- sugar or sweetener (1 tbsp, granulated)
- vinegar (2 tbsp, apple cider)
- kidney beans (1, 15 oz, red)
- puree (3 tsp, tomato)
- garlic (2, crushed)
- tomatoes (1, 15 oz, plum)
- cinnamon (1/2 tsp, ground)
- cumin (1 tsp)
- paprika (1 tsp, smoked)
- onion (1, medium)
- chili (1, red)
- chilies (2, green)
- carrots (2, medium)
- Olive oil
- Mushrooms, as desired

Directions:

1. Finely chop the veggies then lightly fry the mushrooms, onion and garlic then add the other vegetables as you choose.

2. Pour mixture into an oven-proof dish then add the spices and carrots.

3. Set halogen oven to 390 degrees F then cook dish onto lower rack for approx., 20 minutes.

4. Add the sugar, kidney beans and vinegar. Cook at 475 degrees F for roughly 10 minutes. Serve hot.

Marinated Beef Brisket

This tender beef brisket will be a hit for holiday feasts, Sunday dinners or summertime barbeques.

Serves: 4

Time: 2 hours

Ingredients:

- brisket (1, 3-5 lb., corned beef)
- pkt (1, seasoned, purchased with corned beef pkg)
- marinade (your favorite marinade bottled for beef)

Directions:

Place the brisket, after marinating onto a rack then center it. Ensure that it doesn't hang from the sides or touch dome.

If desired, season top of brisket then, place oven dome onto base.

Set to cook for 1 hour at high heat then allow to cook until timer goes off.

Remove the dome from the base then turn the brisket over.

Replace the dome then set timer for approx., 40 more minutes on high heat.

6. Once brisket is done, remove from oven then leave to sit for approx., 15 minutes and then slice. Serve hot.

Roasted Cauliflower

Not everyone enjoys cauliflower raw, even though we know it's a healthy food. Try roasted cauliflower and watch your whole family dig in.

Serves: 2-3

Time: 40 minutes

Ingredients:

- olive oil (2-3 tbsp)
- cauliflower (1 head, large)
- sea salt (1 tsp, coarse)
- black pepper (1/4 tsp, ground)

Directions:

1. Preheat the halogen oven to 400 degrees F then rinse the cauliflower then quarter it.

2. Discard the cores and leaves and cut the quarters into slices ½ inches in thickness.

3. Mix the salt, olive oil, pepper, and cauliflower slices together into zip top bag.

4. Pour cauliflower and seasoning out of bag, spreading them into one layer in baking dish.

5. Bake the cauliflower for 25 minutes. Turning every 10 minutes, Cauliflower will become caramelized or browned.

6. Remove the cauliflower from oven. Serve warm.

Halogen Roasted Chicken

This chicken is very juicy and has a crispy skin and wonderful flavors to entice your family and guests.

Serves: 4-6

Time: 1 & 1/2 hours

Ingredients:

- Olive oil (2 tbsp)
- herbs (1 tsp, mixed)
- chicken (1, large, 5 pounds)
- salt (2 tsp, kosher)
- pepper (1 tsp, ground)

Directions:

1. Wash then pat chicken dry then place it onto lower rack in halogen oven.

2. Mix the herbs, salt, olive oil, and pepper into a small sized bowl. Brush this over the chicken using a pastry brush.

3. Replace the lid onto the oven then set temp to 375 degrees F and timer to 1 hour.

4. Roast chicken until lightly brown to ensure no pink remains.

5. Save the juices from chicken cooking for gravy then mix flour with juice and pour gravy over the chicken. Serve warm.

Swiss Steak

This Swiss Steak is a hearty meal for your guests or just for family.

Serves: 4

Time: 2 hours & 40 minutes

Ingredients:

- broth (1 ½ cups, beef)
- Worcestershire sauce (1 tbsp)
- steak (2 lbs., bottom round)
- tomatoes (1 can, crushed)
- celery stalks (2, chopped)
- garlic cloves (2, minced)
- Vegetable oil to cover bottom of Dutch oven
- Flour (all-purpose, for dredging steak)
- onion (1, sliced, large)
- oregano (1 tsp)
- paprika (1 tsp, smoked)
- black pepper and sea salt (as desired)

Directions:

1. Preheat the halogen oven to 325 degrees F.

2. Tenderize the meat using a meat hammer until slices are 1/4" thick.

3. Place the flour into a pan then mix using sea salt & ground pepper.

4. Dredge the both sides of meat slices then set them aside.

5. Add the vegetable oil to cover bottom of Dutch oven on medium high.

6. When the oil starts shimmering, add the steaks to pan. Don't crowd them.

7. Cook until steaks become browned on each side then remove to plate. Repeat until all steaks are brown.

8. Remove the final steaks from the pot then add the onions, celery, and garlic. Sauté them for approx., two minutes. Add the tomato paste. Combine stirring.

9. Add the beef broth, oregano, Worcestershire sauce, paprika and tomatoes. Combine well.

Return the meat to a pot then submerge in liquid.

Cover the pot then place onto a middle rack of halogen oven. Cook for approx., 1 ½ - 2 hours.

Meat should become quite tender and start to fall apart. Serve promptly.

Sweet Potato Fries

These fries are delicious, and since they are cooked in your halogen oven instead of being deep fried, they're much healthier for you.

Serves: 4

Time: 35 minutes

Ingredients:

- canola oil (1 ½ tbsp)
- potatoes (2, sweet, peeled, wedged, large)
- salt (1/2 tsp, coarse)
- cayenne pepper (2 pinches)

Directions:

1. Preheat the halogen oven to 450 degrees F.

2. Toss the wedges of sweet potato with the canola oil, then the coarse salt and ground pepper.

3. Spread the wedges onto baking sheet then place into halogen oven then bake until wedges become tender and browned. This should approx., 20 minutes or so.

4. Serve warm.

Mushroom Puffs

These delicious appetizers are so easy to make and less time consuming, less time, in your halogen oven.

Serves: 4

Time: 1 hour & 20 minutes

Ingredients:

- chives (2 tbsp, chopped finely)
- mustard (1 tsp, whole grain)
- tomatoes (8, cherry)
- cheese (6 oz, softened)
- egg (1, large)
- mushrooms (4, Portobello)
- Sea salt
- Black pepper (ground)

Directions:

1. Place the baking tray onto top rack of halogen oven then preheat to 340 degrees F for approx., 5 minutes.

2. Remove the stalks then clean mushrooms then separate egg into two small bowls.

3. Beat egg yolk with fork. Add 1 & ¾ ounces of cheese, plus mustard and ½ of chives. Season as desired. Mix well.

4. Spread mushrooms on stalk side with the rest of your cheese. Half cut tomatoes. Place four per each mushroom in cheese topping.

5. Whisk egg white 'til it has stiff peaks. Stir into egg yolk mixture lightly.

6. Place mushrooms on baking tray. Top each with ¼ of egg mixture. Bake at 340F for about 15 to 20 minutes until it is cooked all the way through and browned.

7. Sprinkle on remaining chives. Serve with crusty bread.

Shrimp Scampi

The shrimp cooks very efficiently in a halogen oven and it is truly tasty.

Serves: 6

Time: 1/2 hour

Ingredients:

- breadcrumbs, Japanese (2/3 cup, panko)
- egg (1, large)
- lemon juice (2 tbsp, fresh)
- lemon zest (1 tsp, grated)
- rosemary (1 tsp, fresh, minced)
- Italian parsley (3 tbsp, minced)
- olive oil (3 tbsp)
- butterflied shrimp (4 lbs., peeled,)
- onions (1/4 cup, minced)
- garlic (1 ½ tbsp, minced)
- butter (1 stick, softened)
- wine (2 tbsp, white, dry)
- Sea salt and ground pepper (as desired)
- For serving (lemon wedges)

Directions:

1. Place shrimp into a mixing bowl and gently toss using wine, 1 tsp. of pepper, olive oil, and 1 tsp. of salt then set shrimp aside.

2. Mash the butter, ¼ tsp. of pepper, ½ tsp. of salt, panko, egg yolk, lemon juice, lemon zest, rosemary, parsley, onions and garlic together.

3. Mix well and in an oven-proof, shallow dish, arrange one layer of shrimp then pour the rest of marinade on top of them.

4. Evenly spread butter mixture over the shrimp then bake for approx., 5-7 minutes over high heat until dish becomes bubbly and hot.

5. Serve with lemon wedges.

Garlic Tomatoes

The roasted garlic and roasted tomatoes are a wonderful combination.

Serves: 2

Time: 25 minutes

Ingredients:

- garlic cloves (12)
- tomatoes (1 package, grape)
- tomato (1, oven, with garlic)
- Olive oil
- Salt (coarse)
- Pepper (ground)

Directions:

1. Add your tomatoes into a layer in a baking dish then arrange the garlic evenly using the tomatoes.

2. Drizzle them using oil then sprinkle using salt & pepper.

3. Roast for 20 minutes in 400 degrees F halogen oven. Serve hot.

Asian Beef & Ginger

The beef in this recipe is fork-tender and accompanied by a savory-sweet sauce and plenty of veggies. It's sure to be a hit with your family.

Serves: 6

Time: 1 hour and 40 minutes

Ingredients:

- onion (1/2, bunch, green)
- snap peas (7 oz, halved)
- water (2 tbsp, filtered)
- flour (1 tbsp, corn)
- chili (1/2, tsp, red, dried)
- ginger (1 inch, grated, fresh)
- soy sauce (1 tbsp, dark)
- hot stock (14 oz, vegetable or beef)
- peppers (2, cored, chopped, red)
- celery stalks (2)
- olive oil (3 tbsp)
- braising steak (20 oz, cubed, lean)

Directions:

1. Heat 2 tbsp. of oil into a fry pan on high heat then fry beef until it has browned lightly then transfer it to baking dish.

2. Add the rest of the oil then fry the peppers and celery until they start softening then add them to meat.

3. Pour the stock over meat then add the chilies, soy sauce and ginger. Cover using an aluminum foil and place baking dish onto lower rack of halogen oven.

4. Set oven temperature to 400 degrees F then cook for approx., 45 minutes. Beef should be tender.

5. Blend the water then corn flour then stir into beef then add the green onions and snap peas.

6. Cover then cook for approximately 10 more minutes then serve over rice.

Mexican Quesadillas

This exquisite recipe is one of the most basic kinds of quesadillas that you can make and include such ingredients as cheese, onion, tomato and chili.

Serves: 1-2

Time: 10 minutes

Ingredients:

- Tortillas (2, flour)
- Tomatoes (2 tomatoes, all depending on your own taste)
- Onion (1, white, sliced)
- Cheddar Cheese (sharp, shredded)
- Chili (sliced to your own taste)
- Salt and Pepper (dash)

Directions

1. Using a baking tray (greased), place one floured tortilla upon it.

2. On top of the flour tortilla sprinkle whatever fillings you have chosen. Next you will need to season the quesadilla to your own personal preference.

3. Place the second flour tortilla on top and ensue that you press down upon it firmly.

4. Place the tray onto the high rack then set the temperature to 410 degrees Fahrenheit and cook the quesadilla for only 5-8.

5. Take out your quesadilla then cut into large wedges then serve using the Guacamole, Sour Cream and Salsa and enjoy.

Tuna and Tomato Pasta

This recipe is a delicious dish that every member of your family will love regardless if they are an adult or a child.

Serves: 2

Time: 30 minutes

Ingredients:

- pasta (1 cup)
- Onion (1, small, chopped Finely)
- Butter (2 tbsp)
- Tuna (1 can)
- Italian Passata Tomatoes (1 can)
- Parmesan Cheese (1/2 cup)
- Fresh Basil Leaves (fresh)

Directions:

1. In a pan, boiling the water using a touch of salt and olive oil then cook your pasta over medium heat for approx., 12-15 minutes until the pasta is all done.

2. Once finished, drain the pasta then begin to make the sauce. Chop the onions and sauté them into a small frying pan using some butter and cook until the onions become soft and translucent.

3. Add the pasta then heat for the next 2 minutes and drain tuna then add to your pasta.

4. In a small baking pan add your pasta mixture then sprinkle the top using parmesan cheese.

5. Bake pasta at 400 degrees for approximately 15 minutes until top is a golden brown in color.

6. Add a few fresh basil leaves to garnish then serve and enjoy.

Ham and Cheese Toasted Sandwiches

This tasty recipe is not only easy to make but serves as a quick and easy breakfast or a great tasting snack.

Serves: 4

Time: 15 minutes

Ingredients:

- Bread (8 slices, whole wheat)
- Butter (To spread onto bread)
- Cheddar Cheese (8 slices, sharp)
- Honey Ham (8 slices, Thinly Sliced)
- Mustard (2 tsp)

Directions:

1. You need to assemble your sandwich first. After you have spread butter onto all slices of bread form your sandwich however you want.

2. Add the mustard last before you add the last slice of bread to complete your sandwich.

3. Place sandwiches onto the highest cooking rack then cook your sandwiches into your halogen oven at 480 degrees Fahrenheit until golden brown on both sides.

4. Serve using French fries or potato chips and enjoy.

Delicious Roasted Potatoes

If you have ever wanted to make the most delicious roasted potatoes that will go along with virtually any meat dish that you prepare, this is the perfect recipe for you.

Serves: 4

Time: 55-65 minutes

Ingredients:

- Potatoes (8, red, washed and cubed)
- Sea Salt (dash, Taste)
- Butter (2 tbsp, melted)
- Black Pepper (dash, to Taste)
- Fresh Thyme and Rosemary

Directions:

1. Cut your potatoes (red) after you have washed them into cubes then boil them into water for approx., 5 minutes then drain.

2. Place potatoes into a roasting pan then season using salt, butter and pepper.

3. Add your thyme and rosemary then toss until seasoned fully.

4. Roast in your halogen oven at 480 degrees for approx., 20 minutes.

5. Then reduce heat to 450 degrees Fahrenheit then cook for an additional 40-45 minutes.

6. Lastly, heat the oven back up to 480 degree then cook for another 20 minutes.

7. Remove from heat then allow to cool slightly before serving.

Sweet Bread and Butter Pudding

This is a recipe that you can use to make something delicious with your left-overs.

Serves: 2

Time: 35 minutes

Ingredients:

- Croissants (2)
- Fruit (dried)
- Milk (half pint)
- Sugar (2 tbsp)
- Egg (1)

Directions:

1. Grease a bowl (straight sided) lightly or a small soufflé dish.

2. Slice croissants thinly then set inside your bowl.

3. Sprinkle a bit of the pieces of fruit into your slices.

4. Preheat Halogen oven to 350 degrees Fahrenheit then set your bowl onto the lowest rack.

5. In another bowl add your milk, sugar and egg then whisk until completely blended. Pour mixture over your croissant slices.

6. Add a bit more dried fruit on top of the slices and if you want to sprinkle a touch of cinnamon onto each.

7. Place into your oven and cook for approximately 20 minutes until the insides form a dome shape and are golden brown.

8. Remove from oven then set aside to cool then serve with coffee, tea or a shot of rum then enjoy.

Banana and Carrot Cake

If you have been searching for the most delicious and most cake recipe, you don't have to look any further. This cake includes a perfect combination of both banana and carrot which helps to give this cake the right amount of sweetness and texture. This cake is great to make during the holidays or when you are having a sweet tooth.

Serving Size: 8

Total Cooking and Preparation Time: About 1 hour and 35 minutes

Ingredients:

- 2 Ripe Bananas, Sliced and Mashed
- ¾ cup of Sunflower Oil
- 1/3 cup of Dark Brown Sugar
- 4 Large Eggs, Beaten Lightly
- ¼ cup Carrots, Grated
- 1/4 cup of Sultanas
- ¼ cup Walnuts
- Zest 2 Medium Sized Oranges
- Juice From 1 Orange
- 1 tsp. Baking Soda
- ½ tsp. Baking Powder
- 1 tsp. Ground Cinnamon
- 1-2 cups Flour
- ½ cup Cream Cheese
- 1/3 cup Powdered Sugar
- Lemon Zest

Directions:

1. Lightly grease a cake pan with butter and line the bottom of the pan with a baking sheet. Set aside.

2. Place your mashed banana, eggs, sugar, sultanas, walnuts, carrots, juice and zest into a large mixing bowl and mix until thoroughly combined.

3. Next add the flour, baking soda, baking powder and cinnamon and mix until entire mixture is smooth.

4. Then pour your batter into your cake pan. Place your cake into your halogen oven and back for 35 minutes at 350 degrees.

5. After 35 minutes you will want to turn the temperature down to 320 degrees and continue baking for an additional 30 to 40 minutes until it is done. Use a butter knife to skewer the cake and if the knife comes out clean, your cake is done.

The Icing

1. Beat the powdered sugar, Cream cheese and lemon zest until completely mixed and pipe onto your cake. Serve with ice cream and enjoy.

Mustard Roast Potatoes

Slicing the tops of your potatoes before you cook them will allow the flavors in the fat and other ingredients to be more fully absorbed by the potatoes.

Serves: 4

Time: 90 minutes

Ingredients:

- mustard (1/2 tsp, dried)
- fat (2 tbsp, melted)
- Rosemary and thyme (fresh)
- potatoes (8, large)
- Kosher salt
- Black pepper (ground)

Directions:

1. Peel potatoes then half them lengthways.

2. Parboil into lightly salted water for approx., 5 minutes then drain.

3. Make slits into the potatoes about an inch apart and ¾ of the depth of potato.

4. Place into a roasting tin then drizzle using fat. Sprinkle on pepper, salt, dried mustard, rosemary and thyme.

5. Place onto a low rack of halogen oven on 475 degrees F for approx., 20 minutes. Reduce oven setting to 450 degrees F. Cook for approx., 45 minutes then serve warm.

Spanish Omelet

This Spanish omelet recipe comes with its own hearty goodness, from the fried onions and crispy potatoes.

Serves: 2

Time: 20 minutes

Ingredients:

- cheese (7 oz, feta)
- onion (1, chopped, red)
- eggs (8, beaten, large)
- red peppers (2, chopped)
- potatoes (21 oz, cubed, peeled)

Directions:

1. Preheat halogen oven to 425 degrees F for several minutes then place oven proof dish with a drizzle of olive oil inside to heat the thoroughly dish.

2. Add the potatoes then stir a coat using oil then cook until the potatoes are evenly colored.

3. Add the onion and pepper and a bit more of the olive oil. Coat them evenly, as well. Cook for an additional five more.

4. Remove dish from halogen oven then add beaten eggs then shake to distribute them. Don't stir, since you don't want eggs scrambled yet.

5. Place dish into oven then crumble the cheese on top. Cook for an additional 5 more minutes until dish ingredients are set and golden. Serve hot.

Breakfast Egg Rolls

Give your family the flavors of a good breakfast with this Breakfast Egg Rolls.

Serves: 2-4

Time: 25 minutes

Ingredients:

- egg (1, white)
- garlic (2 tbsp, minced)
- cabbage (1/2 head, shredded)
- bell pepper (1 diced)
- celery stalks (2, sliced)
- carrots (2, shredded)
- onion (1, diced, medium)
- wrappers (1 package, egg roll)
- pork (1 lb., cooked, ground)

Directions:

1. Sauté the garlic and onion for approx., 5 minutes.

2. Add the pork, celery, carrots, cabbage and peppers the sauté for 3-5 more minutes, then season to taste

3. Fill the wrappers with 1/4 to 1/3 of the filling. Seal wrappers with egg white.

4. Place onto rack with the seamed side facing down then repeat until rack is full.

5. Cook for 8-9 minutes on each side. Serve hot.

Caramel Apple Pancakes

These pancakes are delicious as is or can be tweaked to include your favorite ingredients.

Serves: 4

Time: 65 minutes

Ingredients:

- sugar (3 tbsp, granulated)
- apples (3, peeled, quartered, cored, cubed, crisp, sweet, medium)
- cinnamon (1/2 tsp, ground)
- butter (3 tbsp, softened)
- lemon zest (1/4 tsp, grated)
- vanilla extract (1 tsp, pure)
- flour (3/4 cup, whole wheat pastry)
- eggs (3, large)
- milk (3/4 cup, whole)
- Icing sugar (for dusting)
- Sea salt (coarse)

Directions:

1. Preheat halogen oven to 400 degrees F.

2. Blend the eggs and milk into a food processor until mixed well then add the lemon zest, ½ tsp. of salt, cinnamon, vanilla and flour.

3. Blend again until well-combined then cover food processor jar.

4. Place into the refrigerator while you work with the apples.

5. Melt the butter into an oven-safe, non-stick skillet on medium heat. Add the apples then sprinkle with sugar then lower heat to medium-low. Stir apples while cooking until they are softened and browned.

6. Arrange the apples evenly into skillet.

7. Remix the batter into blender jar then pour over the apples.

8. Bake the pancake into halogen oven until set into center and browned. Sides should rise about an inch and a half. This will take approx., 35 minutes.

9. Transfer to a plate then dust using icing sugar. Serve.

Classic Chocolate Cake

This Classic Chocolate Cake is easy and delicious.

Serves: 6

Time: 70 minutes

Ingredients:

- flour (6 oz., sifted, self-rising)
- cocoa (1 tbsp)
- milk (2 tbsp, whole)
- eggs (2, beaten, large)
- butter (3 2/3 oz, softened
- sugar (5 oz, icing)
- sugar (3 ½ oz, granulated)

Directions:

1. Combine the butter and white sugar into a mixing bowl then beat until mixture is fluffy and light.

2. Add the cocoa, milk and eggs and combine well.

3. Add the flour then fold it in until mixture is combined.

4. Grease a baking sheet using non-stick spray then place mixture into a baking sheet then set halogen oven temp to 350 degrees F.

5. Place onto lower grilling rack then bake for 40-50 minutes.

6. Mix several, water drops and icing sugar. It will form a paste for icing. Once your baked cake has cooled cover with the white icing. Serve warm or at room temperature.

Citrus Drizzle Cake

This dish is a favorite for gatherings any time of year.

Serves: 6-8

Time: 30 minutes

Ingredients:

- sugar (3 ½ oz, icing)
- baking powder (1 tsp)
- butter (4 ½ oz., softened)
- eggs (2, medium)
- sugar (4 ¼ oz, caster)
- flour (6 oz, self-rising)
- almonds (2 ¼ oz., ground)
- lemon (1)
- orange (1)

Directions:

1. Remove the lid from the halogen oven then place low rack into oven. Replace the lid hen preheat halogen oven to 350 degrees F.

2. Grate ½ orange and lemon rinds then cut both fruits in halves. Squeeze juice from the fruits until you have 6 tbsp. or so. Mix juices together.

3. Sift baking powder and flour into a medium bowl then break eggs into bowl. Add 3 tbsp. of fruit juice, along with fruit rinds, butter, sugar and almonds.

4. Lightly beat ingredients together until mixed well and fluffy and light. Spoon into your tin. Ensure top surface is level.

5. Place into hot halogen oven then cook for approx., 25 minutes. Cake should rise, be thoroughly cooked and firm to touch.

6. While cake cooks, mix 3 tbsp. of fruit juices and icing sugar into mixing bowl then mix into a paste of smooth consistency.

7. Turn cake out onto a wire rack while it's still hot then make a few holes into the top using a skewer then spoon juice and sugar drizzle over top. Allow to cool. Serve.

Halogen Apple Pie

This is another classic that has been elevated in a halogen oven.

Serves: 6

Time: 40 minutes

Ingredients:

For base:

- pastry mix (16 oz)

For filling:

- sugar (2 ½ oz., caster)

- raisins (2 oz.,)

- nutmeg (1 pinch, grated)

- cinnamon (1 tsp, ground)

- cloves (1 pinch, ground)

- apples (10 oz, cored, chopped)

For top:

- sugar (3/4 oz, caster)

- egg (1 beaten, medium)

Directions:

1. Preheat the halogen oven to 390 degrees F.

2. To make the base: Make the pastry using the directions on the package. Use ¾ of mixture to line one 9-inch pie pan then cut the rest of the pastry into 1/3-inch wide strips.

3. To make the filling: Combine all filling ingredients. Add this to the pie pan you just lined with pastry.

4. To make the topping: Top with pastry strips, forming a lattice shape. Glaze with a bit of egg then sprinkle some sugar on top.

5. Cook onto high rack of your halogen oven for approx., 30 minutes. Serve hot, with cream, custard or ice cream.

Cherry Dump Cake

This dump cake looks and tastes like it took a long time to make, but it's one of the easiest dessert recipes.

Serves: 12

Time: 50 minutes

Ingredients:

- pie filling (1 can, cherry)
- cake mix (1 box, yellow)
- butter (1 stick, softened)
- pineapple (1 can, crushed, partially drained)

Directions:

1. Spray a 13, 9-inch cake pan using non-stick spray.

2. Dump pineapple and the pie filling in the pan then mix it a bit.

3. Sprinkle cake mix over fruit.

4. Slice the butter into thin pieces then place atop cake mix and spread it out.

5. Place the pan in your preheated halogen oven at 375 degrees F. Bake until the mix becomes golden and bubbly.

6. Remove cake from oven then serve with frozen yogurt or ice cream.

Sponge Pudding

This pudding is steamed into a treat that is spongy, simple and sweet.

Serves: 1-2

Time: 1 hour and 45 minutes

Ingredients:

- milk (3 fluid, oz, whole)
- egg (1, beaten)
- sugar (2 oz., caster)
- flour (5 oz, self-rising)
- suet (3 oz)
- syrup (3 fl oz., golden)
- Butter to grease bowl

Directions:

1. Grease a mixing basin then mix ingredients together until they are combined well. Spoon into basin.

2. Cover the basin using two layers of bakery paper then secure them using string. Cover with aluminum foil.

3. Set a basin into halogen cooker bowl then pour boiling water sufficient to go 1/3 up the side of the basin.

4. Heat the halogen oven to 475 degrees Fahrenheit then steam for approx., 1 ½ hour. It should be firm to your touch.

5. Leave into the basin for approx., five minutes, before turning upside down onto serving plate. Serve.

Conclusion

That's it! You've made your way through all 30 easy yet tasty halogen oven recipes for the whole family. I hope you enjoyed all you read and cooked through and that you will be able to keep reusing these Halogen recipes for years to come.

Please take a few minutes to leave a review on the platform on which you got your copy of the book. I would really love to know your feedback.

Until next time!

About the Author

Born in New Germantown, Pennsylvania, Stephanie Sharp received a Masters degree from Penn State in English Literature. Driven by her passion to create culinary masterpieces, she applied and was accepted to The International Culinary School of the Art Institute where she excelled in French cuisine. She has married her cooking skills with an aptitude for business by opening her own small cooking school where she teaches students of all ages.

Stephanie's talents extend to being an author as well and she has written over 400 e-books on the art of cooking and baking that include her most popular recipes.

Sharp has been fortunate enough to raise a family near her hometown in Pennsylvania where she, her husband and children live in a beautiful rustic house on an extensive piece of land. Her other passion is taking care of the furry members of her family which include 3 cats, 2 dogs and a potbelly pig named Wilbur.

Watch for more amazing books by Stephanie Sharp coming out in the next few months.

Author's Afterthoughts

I am truly grateful to you for taking the time to read my book. I cherish all of my readers! Thanks ever so much to each of my cherished readers for investing the time to read this book!

With so many options available to you, your choice to buy my book is an honour, so my heartfelt thanks at reading it from beginning to end!

I value your feedback, so please take a moment to submit an honest and open review on Amazon so I can get valuable insight into my readers' opinions and others can benefit from your experience.

Thank you for taking the time to review!

Stephanie Sharp

For announcements about new releases, please

follow my author page on Amazon.com!

You can find that at:

https://www.amazon.com/author/stephanie-sharp

*or Scan **QR-code** below.*